To Pat:

Woof

Trish Foster

Trish

9/8/2015

Onwards & upwards
x.

Copyright © 2013 Trish Foster

All rights reserved.

ISBN-10: 1482396130
ISBN-13: 978-1482396133

www.kufinnkakennels.com

A dog comes to you and lives with you in your own house,
but you do not therefore own her, as you do not own the rain,
or the trees, or the laws which pertain to them...

A dog can never tell you what she knows from the
smells of the world, but you know, watching her,
that you know almost nothing...

-From "Her Grave"
By Mary Oliver

Dedication

This book is dedicated to the memory of "Kuka,"

my first Finnish Spitz.

Born a Dog, Died a Gentleman

23rdMarch 1995 – 25th June 2010

R.I.P.

Kilconnell Sirma Tovorla "Kuka" Bred by Gerard & Mary Hickey

Acknowledgements

Blessings, love, and hugs to my brother, *author and editor*

Christian de Quincey,

who, with boundless patience, edited and corrected my copious mistakes.

CONTENTS

Dedication	Pg # 4
Acknowledgements	Pg # 5
Introduction	Pg # 7
1. The Basic Commands	Pg # 9
2. Socialization Your New Puppy	Pg # 17
3. Leash and Collar Training	Pg # 26
4. Head Collar Training	Pg # 35
5. Training Collar and Choke Collar	Pg # 38
6. Reward Training	Pg # 41
7. Crate Training	Pg # 45
8. House Training	Pg # 49
Epilogue	Pg # 53
Appendix- The History of the Dog	Pg # 54

Introduction

Getting a new puppy or adult dog is always an exciting time for the entire family.

Dogs are known as man's best friend, and for good reasons. A loyal dog is more than just a pet—he or she quickly becomes a beloved member of the family.
In order to achieve that level of love and companionship, however, it is important to start your puppy or adult dog off on the right foot. A solid grounding in obedience and problem behavior avoidance is essential to making your dog—and you— happier and healthier.

The basis of training any animal is winning its trust, confidence and respect. True training cannot begin until the animal has accepted you as its leader, and totally trusts and respects you.

The most basic dog training is to get your dog to "sit" and "come." They are essential for getting your dog to learn other commands. These commands are used for various reasons—for example, if you are in competition, if your dog jumps making him sit will immediately get him off you or other people, and "come" is the all-important command.

If you take your dog for a walk and you let him of the leash, you expect him to come back to you, not run around the park with you chasing after him shouting at him to "get here right this instant." That would be just downright embarrassing!

While teaching your dog to "come" is one of the most basic of techniques, it also requires a lot of repetition. The simplest way to get him to come is have a toy in one hand and a treat in the other. When you are in the house simply walk away from him, hold out the toy and excitingly call him to you. When he comes over, give him a treat. Always use the same command that you are going to use in the future. Above all, be consistent—your dog expects you to be.

Doing this several times a day is a great way to teach him. But remember to have lots of long breaks so he doesn't get bored and stops enjoying the interaction with you. And don't forget the treats!

Getting your dog to sit could be slightly harder, but again requires only basic dog training. When you have mastered the "come" command, call him to you, place your hand on the end of his back and say "Sit," while gently pushing down on his backside. When he sits his bottom down, give him a treat and a lot of praise.

If you want him to sit longer, just delay giving him the treat and the praise, get him to sit but take your time bending down to him and feeding him his tidbit. Basic dog training is simple and very effective. It should also be fun for you and your dog, it doesn't have to be hours and hours each day just may be five minutes or so.

Don't forget to reward your dog and yourself for all the "hard" work, though!!
Let's start with basic puppy training. In the next chapter, we will cover the basics from bringing the new addition home to making sure he is properly socialized and well behaved.

Chapter 1
The Basic Commands

There are, of course, many reasons for owners to want a calm, obedient, and faithful dog. Obedient and well-trained dogs are happier dogs, less likely to get into tussles with people or other dogs.

And, of course, training your dog well will also make him or her a much better family companion, especially in households with young children.

Many studies have shown that proper dog training makes a big impact when it comes to reducing and managing behavior problems encountered by dog-owning households.

When considering training your own dog, or having someone else help you train it, you need to master six basic commands in order for your dog to be considered truly trained.

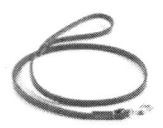

The Six Basic Commands

Heel — Every dog should learn to walk beside its owner on a loose leash, neither pulling ahead nor lagging behind

No — Every dog should learn to respond to the word "No." (This tiny but important word can save you a ton of trouble.)

Sit — Training your dog to sit on command is a vital part of any dog training program.

Stay — A well-trained dog should remain where his or her owner commands. That's why "Stay" is a very important command in dog training.

Down — Lying down on command is more than just a cute trick. It is a key component of any successful dog training program.

Off — This is another vital command to ensure the safety of people and your dog.

Every dog should know these six commands—"Heel", "No", "Sit", "Stay", "Down," and "Off".

These six commands are the foundation of every basic obedience class, and it is vital that you and your dog master these basic commands.

These are the fundamentals, and it will be impossible to move onto other commands, or to correct behavior problems, without having mastered the basics.

Let's start with the most basic command of all:

The 'Heel' Command

Teaching a dog to heel is the fundamental first step in teaching him to walk properly on the leash. The proper place for the dog to walk is at your side, neither lagging behind nor straining to get ahead.

If your dog begins to forge ahead, gently tug on the leash. This will cause the training collar to tighten and give the dog a gentle reminder to fall back into line. If he begins to lag behind, gently urge him forward. A lure or toy is a good tool for the dog that constantly lags behind.

Once the dog is consistently walking at your side, try to change your pace and encouraging him to match his pace with yours. It should always be the dog who adjusts his pace to yours. You should never adjust your pace to meet the needs of the dog.

The 'No' Command

The word "no" is important for your dog to learn, and one you may use a lot as training begins.
It is important that the dog learn to respond to a sharp 'No' promptly and obediently.

Keep the sharp 'No' command when your dog does not respond to the 'Off', or 'Down" command.

The 'Sit' Command

The "Sit" command is another vital element in dog training. Teaching a dog to sit, using voice commands alone, will form the groundwork of much future training, so it is important for the dog (and you) to master this vital skill.

You can combine the "Sit" with the "Heel command. As you walk alongside your dog, stop abruptly. If she does not stop when you do, give a sharp tug on the leash to remind her. Many dogs will instinctively stop when you do, while others need to be reminded through the use of the leash and the training collar.

Once the dog has stopped by your side, urge her to sit by pushing gently on her hindquarters. Don't use too much pressure, or push her down abruptly. Doing so could frighten, or even injure the dog. Rather, apply a steady downward pressure. Most dogs will recognize this as a "Sit" command. It is important to say the word "Sit" as you do this.

Repeat this procedure a few times by walking, stopping, and sitting your dog.
After a few repetitions, she will probably begin to sit down on her own every time she stops. Once more: It is important to say the word "Sit" each time, so that the dog will eventually learn to respond to voice commands alone.

The 'Stay' Command

Like "Sit," the "Stay" command is a vital building block to other, more advanced training. For instance, "Stay" is vital to teaching your dog to come when called, which, in turn, is vital for off-leash work.

"Stay" can be made into an extension of the "Sit" command. Have your dog sit, and while she is sitting, slowly back away. If she begins to follow you, as she probably will at first, come back to the dog and ask her to sit again. Repeat the process until you can reach the end of the leash without your dog getting up from a sitting position.

After the dog reliably stays where you indicate, you can try dropping the leash and backing away further. It will probably take the dog some time to reliably stay where she is put without becoming distracted.

The 'Down' Command

"Down" is another important part of any basic obedience training program.

Teaching a dog to lie down on command is much more than an entertaining trick. The down command is very important for regaining control of a dog, or stopping one that is engaged in an inappropriate behavior.

Have your dog get into the sitting position and depending on the size of your dog stand or kneel right next to him.

To coax and guide your dog into the "down" position, with one hand holding the leash, gently pull the dog's head down towards the ground giving the "down" command as you are doing so. At the same time place your free hand between the shoulder blades and keep pressing down gently. Keep repeating "down" until the dog is down.

As soon as you have the dog in the down position immediately reward him and let him know what a super dog he is.

You can also lift up your dog's front legs once in the "sit" position and by extending them out in front of him towards you, he will lie down. Adopt the method which works best for you and be sure to praise and encourage your dog all the way down and reward him.

After lots of repetition your dog will respond to your verbal command only. Then try the command when your dog is in the standing position and in other settings.

The 'Off' Command

The "Off" command is just as vital as the other commands, and it forms the basis for later training, especially when training the dog not to chase people, cars, bikes, cats, etc.

For instance, to train a dog to remain still when a bicycle goes by, you would stand with the dog calmly on the leash. If she begins to strain against the leash, sharply issue an "Off" command accompanied by a tug of the leash. Eventually, the dog will learn to respond to the voice command alone.

Proper dog training does much more than just creating an obedient, willing companion. It actually strengthens the bond that already exists between dog and handler.

Dogs are pack animals, and they look to their pack leader to tell them what to do. The key to successful dog training is to establish that you are the pack leader.

Becoming the "pack leader" is a very important concept for any potential dog trainer to understand. There is only one leader in every pack of dogs, and the owner must establish him or herself as the dominant animal. Failure to do so will lead to all manner of behavior problems.

A properly trained dog will respond to all the owner's commands, and will not display anxiety, displeasure, or confusion. A good dog training program will focus on allowing the dog to learn just what is expected of him or her, and will use positive reinforcement to reward desired behaviors.

In addition to making the dog a good member of the community, obedience training is a great way to fulfill some of the dog's own needs—including the need for exercise, the security that comes with knowing what is expected of it, a feeling of accomplishment, and a good working relationship with its handler.

Dog training gives the dog an important job to do, and an important goal to reach.

Giving your dog a job is more important than you may think. Dogs were originally bred by humans to do important work, such as herding sheep, guarding property, and protecting people.

Many dogs today have no important job to do, and this can often lead to boredom and neurotic behavior. Basic obedience training and on-going training sessions provide the dog with a job to do. This is especially important for high energy breeds like German shepherds and border collies.

Training sessions are a great way for these high energy dogs to use up their extra energy and to simply enjoy themselves.

Incorporating playtime into your dog training sessions is a great way to prevent both you and your dog from becoming bored.

Remember playing with your dog helps to strengthen the all-important bond between your dog and you as the pack leader.

Chapter 2
Socializing Your New Puppy

Photo courtesy Steve and Alison Piearce – Sukunimi Finnish Spitz

Bringing a new puppy into the household is always an exciting and fun time. Everyone wants to play with, cuddle, and hold the little ball of fur. The last thing on the minds of most new puppy owners is training the new addition to the family, but it is important that puppy training and socialization begin as early as possible.

In some ways, training a puppy is easier than training an adult or adolescent dog. One reason is that the puppy is essentially a "blank slate," untroubled by past training techniques and other issues. In other ways, however, the puppy can be more difficult to train than an older dog.

One challenge to training a new puppy is that they are more easily distractible than adolescent and adult dogs. Everything is new to a puppy, and every new experience provides a new chance for distraction. For this reason, it is best to keep training sessions short when working with a puppy, and to end each training sessions on a positive note.

Socialization

Socializing a new puppy is a vital part of any training program, and it is important for socialization to begin early. The window for socialization is very short, and a puppy that is not properly socialized to people, dogs, and other animals by the time he or she is four-months old often never develops the socialization he or she needs to become a good canine citizen.

Socialization training is vital to making your new puppy a good canine citizen, as dog aggression is a growing problem in many areas.

A properly socialized dog learns how to play properly with other dogs, and overly aggressive play is punished by the other dogs in the play group. This type of play learning is something that happens among siblings in litters of puppies. As the puppies play with each other, they learn what is appropriate and what is not.

Inappropriate behavior, such as hard biting or scratching, is punished by the other puppies, by the mother dog, or both. Unfortunately, many puppies are removed from their mothers and sold or adopted before this socialization has fully occurred.

Therefore, puppy play sessions are a very important part of any puppy training session. Most good puppy preschool training programs provide time in each session for this type of dog interaction. Introducing your puppy to new experiences and new locations is also an important part of puppy training. Teaching your dog to be obedient and responsive, even in the face of many distractions, is very important when training dogs and puppies. One great way to socialize your puppy both to new people and new dogs is to take it on a trip to your local pet store.

Many major pet store chains, and some independent ones as well, allow pet parents to bring their furry children, and these stores can be great places for puppies to get used to new sights, sounds, and smells. Of course you will want to make sure the store allows pets before heading over. Learning how to interact with other dogs is something that normally would occur between littermates. However, since most dogs are removed from their mothers so soon, this littermate socialization often does not finish properly.

One vital lesson puppies learn from their littermates and from the mother dog is how to bite, and how not to bite. Puppies naturally roughhouse with each other, and their thick skin protects them from most bites. However, when one puppy bites too hard, the other puppies, or the mother dog, quickly reprimand him, often by holding him by the scruff of his neck until he submits.

The best way to socialize your puppy is to have it play with lots of other puppies. It is also fine for the puppy to play with a few adult dogs, as long as they are friendly and well socialized.

Many communities have puppy playschool and puppy kindergarten classes. These classes can be a great way to socialize any puppy, and for handler and puppy alike to learn some basic obedience skills.

When socializing puppies, it is best to let them play on their own and work out their own issues when it comes to appropriate roughness of play. The only time humans should step in is if one puppy is hurting another, or if a serious fight breaks out. Other than that, people should simply stand back and watch their puppies interact.

While this socialization is taking place, the pack hierarchy should quickly become apparent. Some puppies are ultra-submissive, rolling on their backs and baring their throats at the slightest provocation. Other puppies in the class will be dominant, ordering the other puppies around and telling them what to do. Watching the puppies play, and determining what type of personality traits your puppy has, will be very valuable in determining the best way to proceed with more advanced training. As the socialization process proceeds, of course, it will be necessary to introduce the puppy to all sorts of humans as well as all sorts of puppies.

Fortunately, the puppy kindergarten class makes this process quite easy, since every puppy gets to interact with every human. It is important that the puppy be exposed to men, and women, older people, and children, and a variety of ethnicities. Dogs do not see every human as the same. To a dog, a man and a woman are completely different animals. It is also important to introduce the puppy to a variety of other animals, especially in a multi pet household.

Introducing the puppy to friendly cats is important, as are introductions to other animals the puppy may encounter, such as rabbits, guinea pigs and the like.

If your household contains a more exotic creature, it is important to introduce the puppy to it as early as possible, but to do it in a way that is safe for both animals.

It is often best to start by introducing the puppy to the smell of the other animals. This can easily be accomplished by placing a piece of the animal's bedding, such as a towel or bed liner, near where the puppy sleeps. Once the puppy is accustomed to the smell of the other creature; he or she is much more likely to accept the animal as another member of the family.

It is important for puppy owners to structure their pet's environment so that the puppy is rewarded for good behaviors and not rewarded for others. One example of this is jumping on people. Many people inadvertently reward this behavior because it can be cute. While it is true that jumping can be cute for a 10-pound puppy, it will not be so cute when that puppy has grown into a 100-pound dog.

Instead of rewarding the puppy for jumping, try rewarding it for sitting. This type of positive reinforcement will result in a well behaved adult dog that is a valued member of both the family and the community at large.

This type of reinforcement can also be used in potty training the new puppy. For instance, teaching him to use a unique surface such as gravel or asphalt is a good technique. The theory is that the puppy will associate this surface with doing potty, and therefore be reluctant to use other surfaces (like your kitchen carpet for instance).

It is best to introduce a new puppy to the household when everyone in the family is present, and when the household is as calm as possible. That is why animal care experts discourage parents from giving puppies and kittens as holiday gifts. The holiday season is typically much too busy, with far too many distractions, for a young puppy or kitten to get the attention it needs. It is best to wait until the holidays have passed before introducing the new family member.

Once the puppy is part of the household, you will begin to notice signs of what he or she will need to learn. One of the first challenges of a multi-story home will be learning to climb up and down the stairs. Many puppies are afraid of stairs, and that usually means they do not know how to climb them properly. It is important for the puppy's owner to slowly build the dog's confidence, starting off at the bottom of the stairs. In general, a wide stairway will probably be less frightening to the puppy.

To build confidence, you should go up the first step, and then encourage your puppy to join you, using your voice, treats, or a toy. After the puppy has joined you on the first stair, go back down and repeat the process until the puppy will go up that step on her own. It is important to build confidence slowly and not rush the process. Taking a one-step-at-a-time approach is the best way to teach your puppy to not be afraid.

Collar Training

Another thing every new puppy must learn is how to accept the collar. Learning to wear a collar is important to every dog, but many puppies are baffled, frightened, and bewildered by this new piece of equipment, and try desperately to remove it by pawing and pulling at it.

When choosing a collar for your new puppy, make sure it fits properly. A well-fitting collar is more likely to be comfortable and accepted.

While choke, slip, and training collars can be good training aids, they should never be used as a substitute for a sturdy buckle-type collar.

And, of course, that collar should have an identification tag and license attached. This identification will be vital in getting your puppy back if she gets lost.

Puppies should be micro-chipped at eight weeks!

The best way to introduce your puppy to the collar is to simply put it on and allow her to squirm, jump, roll, and paw at it to her heart's content. It is important not to encourage this behavior by trying to soothe her, but it is just as important not to punish or reprimand your puppy, either.

The best strategy is to simply ignore the puppy and let her work through her issues with the collar on her own. Introducing distractions, such as food, toys, or playing is a good way to get the puppy used to the collar. Getting the puppy to play, eat, and drink while wearing the collar is a great way to get her used to it. After a few days, most puppies will not even know they are wearing a collar.

Teaching Your Puppy Proper Socialization Skills

Teaching a puppy or adult dog good socialization skills is vital to the safety of both your dog and other dogs and people he comes into contact with. A properly socialized dog is a happy dog, and a joy to be around for both humans and other animals. A poorly socialized dog, or one with no socialization at all, is a danger to other animals, other people—even his own family.

Socialization lessons are best done when the puppy is as young as possible. Once learned, socialization of a young puppy is difficult to undo, and it is important to remember that the socialization skills the puppy learns will affect his behavior for the rest of his life.

A dog that is properly socialized will be neither frightened of nor aggressive toward other animals, including humans.

A properly socialized dog will take each new experience and stimulus in stride, and not become fearful or aggressive. Dogs that are not properly socialized often bite because of fear, and such a dog can become a hazard and a liability to the family it lives with. Improperly socialized dogs are also unable to adapt to new situations. A routine matter like a trip to the vet or to a friend's house can quickly stress the dog out and lead to all sorts of problems.

Socialization is best done when the puppy is very young, perhaps around 12 weeks. Even after 12 weeks, however, it is important that the puppy continues its socialization in order to refine the all-important social skills. It is possible to socialize an older puppy, but it is very difficult to achieve after the all-important 12 week period has passed.

Now let's look at some definite "Dos" and "Don'ts" for socializing any puppy. Let's start with what the "Dos." we will explore what to avoid a little later.

Socialization 'Dos' . . .

Make each socialization event as pleasant and non-threatening for the puppy as possible. If your puppy's first experience with any new situation is unpleasant, it will be very difficult to undo in the puppy's mind. In some cases, an early trauma can morph into a phobia that can last a lifetime. It is better to take things slow and avoid having the puppy become frightened or injured.

Invite your friends over to meet the new puppy. It is important to include as many different people as possible in the puppy's circle of acquaintances, including men, women, children, adults, as well as people of many diverse ethnic backgrounds and ages.
Also invite friendly and healthy dogs and puppies over to meet your puppy. It is important for the puppy to meet a wide variety of other animals, including cats, hamsters, rabbits, and other animals he is likely to meet. It is of course important to make sure that all animals the puppy comes into contact with have received all necessary vaccinations.

Take the puppy to many different places, including shopping centers, pet stores, parks, school playgrounds and on walks around the neighborhood. Try to expose her to places with crowds of people and lots of activity going on.

Take the puppy for frequent short rides in the car. Be sure to stop the car once in a while and let the puppy look out the window at the world outside.

Introduce your puppy to a variety of items that may be unfamiliar. The puppy should be exposed to common items like bags, boxes, vacuum cleaners, umbrellas, hats, etc. that may be frightening to him. Allow and encourage the puppy to explore these items and see that he has nothing to fear from them.

Get the puppy used to a variety of objects by rearranging familiar items. Simply placing a chair upside down or placing a table on its side creates an object that your puppy will perceive as totally new.

Get the puppy used to common procedures like being brushed, bathed, having her nails clipped, teeth cleaned, ears cleaned, etc. Your groomer and your veterinarian will thank you for this.

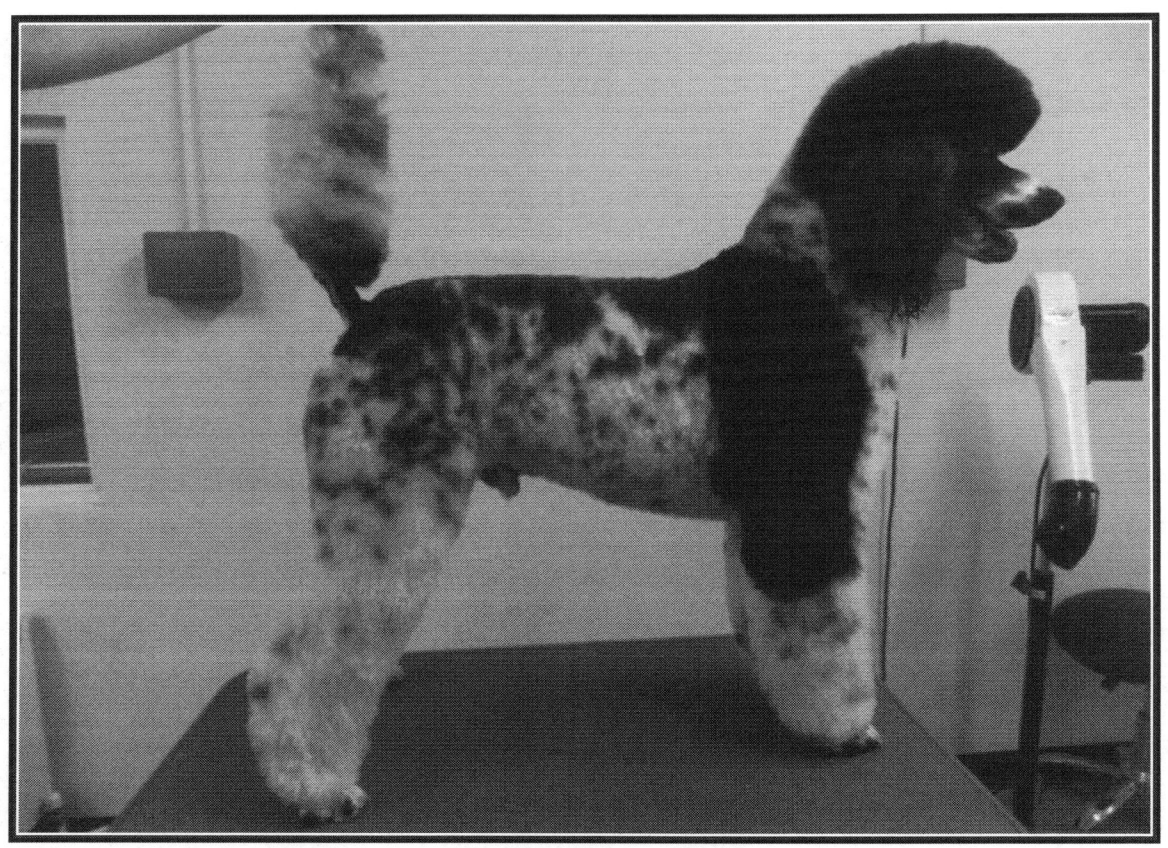

"Yogi" Owned by Leonie Fahy – Canine Grooming Sallins.

Of course, you should also avoid some things when socializing a puppy.

. . . and 'Don'ts'

Do not place the puppy on the ground when strange animals are present. An attack, or even a surprise inspection, by an unknown animal could traumatize the puppy and hurt his socialization.

Do not inadvertently reward fear-based behavior. When the puppy shows fear, it is normal to try to soothe it, but this could reinforce fear-based behavior and make it worse. Since biting is often a fear reaction, reinforcing fear can create problems with biting.

Do not force or rush the socialization process. It is important to allow the puppy to socialize at his own pace.

Do not try to do too much too soon. Young puppies have short attention spans, and continuing lessons after that attention span has passed will be a waste of your time and your puppy's.

Do not wait too long to begin. You have a short window in which to begin the socialization process.

A young puppy is a blank slate, and it is important to fill that slate with positive socialization skills as early as possible.

Chapter 3
Leash and Collar Training

There are many different styles of dog training, and finding the one that works best for you is important for creating a dog that is a talented, loyal, and faithful member of the family. All successful methods of dog training work to reinforce the relationship between dog and handler, and the foundation of any successful training program is getting the respect of the dog.

Fortunately, dogs are wired by nature to seek out leaders, and to follow the direction of those leaders.

Both leash/collar training and reward training have been around for a very long time, and they have proven their effectiveness over time. The type of training that works best will vary from dog to dog, and from breed to breed.

It is important to remember that each breed of dog has its own unique qualities, reinforced by hundreds of years of selective breeding.

Of course personalities of individual dogs vary quite a bit, even within established breeds.

You, as the handler of the dog, know better than anyone about which style of dog training will work best, so it is important to work with the trainer you choose to achieve your goal of a willing, obedient and friendly dog. Leash and collar training is the best way to accomplish many types of dog conditioning, particularly in situations where the dog must have a high level of reliability.

For instance, dogs that have an important job to do, such as rescue dogs, police dogs, and guard dogs, generally benefit from leash and collar training. In leash and collar training, varying degrees of force can be used, ranging from slight prompts with the lead to very harsh corrections.

The amount of correction used should be appropriate to the situation, since using too much, or too little correction will be ineffective. In a collar-and-leash based dog training program, first the dog is taught a particular behavior, generally with the leash.

After the dog has demonstrated that it understands the command, the leash is then used to correct the dog if it disobeys, or when it makes a mistake.

The leash is the main form of controlling and communicating with the dog in leash-and-collar training. When using leash-and-collar training, the dog must be trained to trust the handler and accept directions without question. In order for the dog to be fully trained, the handler must demonstrate the ability to place the dog into a posture or position he does not want to take.

This does not mean using force, but it does generally require some level of physical manipulation.

This manipulation is most easily and safely done using the main tool of leash and collar training—the leash. It is important for every dog trainer to understand that the leash is simply a tool. While the leash is important in this form of training, it is important for the dog trainer to also be able to eventually achieve the same results using whatever tools are at hand.

Even when the only tools available are the handler's body and skill, the dog should be willing to obey. Creating a leader/follower relationship between handler and dog is crucial, and it is important to use the leash as a tool and not a crutch.

A properly trained dog should be willing to obey whether the leash is present or not. The leash and training collar is the most basic piece of equipment used in for dog training. Using the leash and training collar properly is vital for success with your puppy.

The training collar is designed to apply a specific amount of pressure each time the leash is tightened. The amount of pressure put on the leash controls the amount of pressure placed on the training collar, and the pressure can be adjusted according to how the dog responds. How each dog responds to training with the leash and collar varies from dog to dog.

Some puppies barely react the first time they encounter a collar and leash, while others fight this strange contraption with all their might. It is important to recognize how your own dog reacts, and to adapt your training program as needed. The first part of training with collar and leash, of course, is to purchase a quality, well- made training collar that will fit your dog properly.

There are many types of training collars and leashes on the market. The most important thing is to choose one that is sturdy and well made. The last thing you want to do is chase your dog down after he has broken his collar. The collar should be approximately two inches longer than the circumference of the dog's neck. It is important to get an accurate size using a measuring tape—making sure that the tape is not tight around the dog's neck.

Most training collars come in even sizes, so you should round up to the next size if your dog's neck is an odd number. It is important that the chain that attaches to the collar be placed at the top of the dog's neck. That is where the training collar is designed to apply the best pressure.

The ability to apply varying degrees of pressure, and to relieve that pressure instantly, is what makes a training collar such an effective tool. It usually takes new users a little while to get used to using the training collar, and some styles of training collar require more finesse than others.

If you are unsure which collar to choose, be sure to ask a professional dog trainer or the management staff at your local pet store for help. After you have become familiar with the way the training collar works, it is time to begin using it to train your dog to walk properly on a leash.

A well-trained dog is one who will walk at his handler's side on a loose leash, neither dropping behind nor charging ahead.

A well-trained dog will also vary her pace to meet her handler's stride.

Under no circumstances should the handler be forced to change pace to match the dogs. If the dog does begin to charge ahead, be sure to promptly correct this by giving a quick tug on the leash. This will give the dog a good reminder that she needs to change pace. It is important to quickly relieve the pressure as soon as the dog responds. The training collar is designed to relieve pressure as soon as the leash is loosened.

Most dogs will immediately respond to corrections by a good, properly used training collar. If the dog does not respond as directed, it may be necessary to apply greater pressure. This can be especially true of large dogs or those who have pre-existing behavior or control problems. If you are still unable to get a response from your dog, it is possible that you are using a training collar that is not large enough for your dog. If you think this may be the case, be sure to ask for expert advice before proceeding.

The Training Collar

Getting your puppy to walk with collar and leash is the basis of all further training. Until your dog has learned to accept the collar and leash, it will be impossible to perform any additional training.

After you have purchased the perfect collar, the next step is to put it on the dog and allow him to wear it around the house. Do not be dismayed if the dog whines, paws at the collar or otherwise tries to remove it. This is normal, and the dog should not be punished for it. It is best to simply ignore the dog and allow him to work out his own issues with the collar. Your puppy should be allowed to wear the collar 24 hours a day for a number of days to get used to how it feels on his neck. After the dog accepts the collar well, it is time to start introducing the leash. A lightweight leash works best for this process.

The Training Leash

Simply attach the leash to your dog's collar and allow her to walk around the house with it. Of course, she should be supervised during this process in order to make sure she doesn't get the leash caught on anything. A snagged leash could frighten the dog and create "leash phobia" that would be hard to overcome later. In the beginning, the leash should be attached only for a few minutes at a time.

Be sure to attach the leash at happy times, such as playtime, meal time, etc. It is important for the dog to associate the leash with happy things. When the leash is not attached to the dog, it is a good idea to keep it near the dog's food and water bowls. Your puppy should be encouraged to investigate her leash, and to discover that it isn't something to fear. After she is comfortable walking around the house wearing the leash, it is time for you to pick up the end of the leash for a few minutes.

You should not try to walk the puppy on the leash; simply hold the end of the leash and follow the puppy around as she walks around. You should try to avoid situations where the leash becomes taut; and any pulling or straining on the leash should be avoided. It is fine for the puppy to sit down. Try a few games with the collar and leash.

For instance, back up and encourage the puppy to walk toward you. Do not drag her towards you; simply encourage her to come. If she does, praise her profusely and reward with a food treat or toy.

You should always strive to make all the time spent on the leash as pleasant as possible. Give the puppy plenty of practice getting used to walking on the leash in the home. It is best to do plenty of work in the home, since it is a safe environment with few distractions.

After the puppy is comfortable walking indoors on a leash, it is time to start going outside, beginning of course in a small, enclosed area like a fenced yard. After the puppy has mastered walking calmly outdoors on a leash, you can then visit some places with more distractions.

You may want to start with a place like a neighbor's yard.

Walking your new puppy around the neighborhood is a good way to introduce your neighbors to the new puppy, while giving the puppy valuable experience in avoiding distractions and focusing on his leash training. Puppies sometimes develop bad habits with their leashes, such as biting or chewing on it. To discourage this, try applying a little bit of bitter apple, Tabasco sauce or similar substance (just make sure the substance you use is not toxic to dogs). This strategy usually convinces puppies that chewing the leash is a bad idea.

Training Your Dog to Not Pull On the Leash

Pulling on the leash is one of the most common misbehaviors with all kinds of dogs. Puppies and adult dogs alike can often be seen taking their handlers for walks, instead of the other way around. Pulling on the leash can be much more than an annoying habit. Leash pulling can lead to a broken collar or leash, allowing your dog to escape. An out-of-control, off-leash dog can be both destructive and dangerous to itself and to others. Leash pulling can result from a variety of different things. In some cases, the dog may simply be so excited to go for a walk that she is unable to control herself. In other cases, the dog sees himself as the leader of the pack, and he simply takes the "leadership position" at the front of the pack.

If leash-pulling is the result of excitement, simply giving your dog a few minutes to calm down can often be a big help. Simply stand with your dog on the leash for a couple minutes and let the initial excitement of the upcoming walk pass. After the initial excitement has worn off, many dogs are willing to walk calmly on their leash.

If the problem is one of control, however, some retraining may be in order. All dog training starts with the owner establishing him or herself as the alpha dog, or pack leader, and without this basic respect and understanding, no effective training can occur. For dogs exhibiting these types of control issues, a step back to basic obedience commands is in order. These dogs can often be helped through a formal obedience school structure.

A good dog trainer will insist on working with the handler as well as the dog. Calmly accepting the collar and lead is the basis of teaching your dog to walk.

A dog that jumps up and down while the collar is being put on will not walk properly. Begin by asking him to sit down, and insisting that he sit still while the collar is put on. If he begins to get up, or gets up on his own after the collar is on, be sure to sit him back down immediately. Begin the walk only after the dog sits calmly to have the collar put on, and continues to sit calmly as the leash is attached.

Once the leash is attached, it is important to make the dog walk calmly toward the door. If she jumps or surges ahead, gently correct her with a tug of the leash and return her to a sitting position. Make the dog stay and then move on again. Repeat this process until the dog is walking calmly by your side.

Repeat the above process when you reach the door. The dog should not be allowed to surge out of the door, or to pull you through the open door. If the dog begins this behavior, return him to the house and make him sit quietly until he can be trusted to walk through the door properly. Starting the walk with you in control is vital to creating a well-mannered dog. As you begin your walk, be sure to keep your dog's attention focused on you at all times.

Remember, the dog should look to you for guidance, not take the lead himself. When walking, it is important to stop often. Every time you stop, your dog should stop, too.

Getting into the habit of asking your dog to sit down every time you stop is a good way to keep her attention focused on you. Make sure she is looking at you, and then move off again. If she begins to surge ahead, immediately stop and ask her to sit. Repeat this process until the dog reliably stays at your side. Each time the dog does what you ask, reward her with a treat, a toy, or just your praise. Remember, if your dog pulls on the leash and you continue to walk him anyway, you are inadvertently rewarding unwanted behavior.

Dogs learn whether you are teaching them or not, and learning the wrong things now will make learning the right things later that much harder. It is important to be consistent in your expectations. Every time the dog begins to pull ahead, immediately stop and make the dog sit. Continue to have the dog sit quietly until his focus is solely on you. Then start out again, making sure to immediately stop moving if he surges ahead.

Off-Leash Training

Many dog handlers are anxious to give their four-legged companions the freedom of going off leash, but it is important not to rush that important step. Dogs should be allowed off leash only after they have become masters of all the basic obedience commands, such as walking at your heel, sitting, and staying on command.

Another skill that must be completely mastered before the dog can be taken off the leash is the "come when called" command. Even if the dog can heel, sit, and stay perfectly, if he cannot be relied on to come when called, he is not ready to be taken off the leash. Taking any dog off the leash, especially in a busy, crowded area, or one with a lot of traffic, is a big step and not one to be taken lightly. Make sure you adequately test your dog in a safe environment before taking him off his leash.

After all, the leash is the main instrument of control. You must be absolutely certain you can rely on your voice commands for control before removing the leash. Keep your dog on a leash in areas where you are requested to do so!

Always carry poop bags with you in case you need one. After the dog has been trained to understand the "Sit," "Stay," and "Come" commands, it is important to challenge the dog with various distractions.

It is a good idea to start by introducing other people, other animals, or both, while the dog is in a safe environment like a fenced in yard. Have a friend or neighbor stand just outside the fence while you hold your dog on the leash. As the friend or family member walks around the outside of the fence, watch your dog's reactions closely. If he starts to pull at the leash, quickly tug him back.

Repeat this exercise until the dog will reliably remain at your side. After this, you can try dropping the leash, and eventually removing it, and repeating the distraction. It is important to vary the distractions, such as introducing other animals, other people, traffic, rolling balls, etc. After your dog is able to remain still in the face of distraction, start introducing the "come when called" lessons with distractions in place.

Invite some of your neighbors to bring their dogs over to play with yours. As the dogs romp in the fenced-in yard, try calling your dog. When he comes to you, immediately give him lots of praise, and perhaps a food reward. After he has been rewarded, immediately allow him to go back to playing. Repeat this several times throughout the day, making sure each time to reward the dog and immediately allow him to go back to his fun.

After your puppy has seemingly mastered coming when called in his own yard, try finding a local dog park or similar area where you can practice with the command. Initially find a small area or to choose a fenced-in patch, in case you lose control of the dog.
If you cannot find a fenced-in area, choose a place well away from people and cars. Practice with your dog by allowing him to play with other dogs, or just to sniff around, and then call him to you.

When he comes, immediately reward and praise him, then let him resume his previous activities. Doing this will teach the dog that coming to you is the best option and the one most likely to bring both rewards and continued good times.

Only after your dog has consistently demonstrated the ability to come when called, even when there are many distractions around, is it safe to allow her time off leash. Off-leash time should never be unsupervised.

For both your well-being and your dog's, at all times make sure you know where he is and what he is doing.

It is easy for a dog to get into trouble quickly, so you should always keep an eye on him, whether he is chasing squirrels in the park, playing with other dogs, or just chasing a ball with the neighbor's kids.

Chapter 4
Head Collar Training

The Halti Head Collar

Over the past few years, the head collar has become an increasingly popular dog training tool.

Two of the most well-known brands are The Gentle Leader and The Halti, but there are many other brands on the market that incorporate the basic head collar concept.

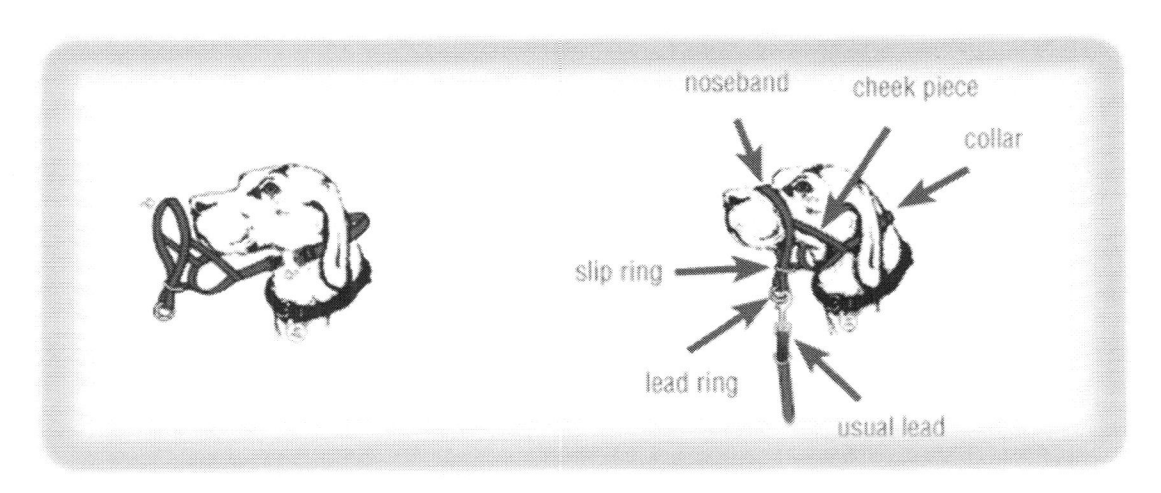

The Gentle Leader is designed to fasten around the dog's neck.

The advantage of this design is that even if the dog is somehow able to wriggle out of the muzzle, it is still wearing a collar. This safety feature is very important, especially during training outside or in novel situations. On the other hand, the Halti offers better control of the dog, and for this reason it is often favored when working with aggressive dogs.
Training a dog with a head collar has a number of advantages over training with a traditional or training collar. For one thing, head collars are often easier to use for beginning dog trainers than are training collars. Head collars are also quite effective at preventing dogs from pulling, or controlling and for retraining dogs that tend to pull.

The Gentle Leader

Many people find The Gentle Leader easier to fit than The Halti.

Head collars can also be quite effective at controlling dogs in difficult situations, such as a dog that wants to be with other dogs. Most handlers know of some situations in which their dogs are difficult to control, and head collars can be quite effective at taking charge of these volatile situations.

Head collars can be excellent for controlling dogs that are very strong, or for working with a dog in an area that contains a great many distractions. For instance, head collars are great for when your dog is on an outing, or in an area where other dogs are likely to be distractions.

Even though a head collar can be a great tool, it should not be used as a replacement for effective dog training. A head collar is most effective when it is used in combination with strong and sensible dog training methods, such as reward training and other forms of positive reinforcement.

Disadvantages of Head Collars

Even though head collars have many advantages, they have some distinct disadvantages as well.

For one thing, head collars tend to make many dogs dependent on the equipment, and they quickly learn the difference between their regular collar and the head collar, and adjust their behavior accordingly.

In addition, some dogs—particularly those not accustomed to wearing a head collar—dislike wearing it and paw at it, try to rub it off or pull excessively. If your dog exhibits this behavior, the best strategy is to keep it moving until he or she learns to accept the collar. A good alternative is to have the dog sit by pulling up on the dog's head.

Another disadvantage of the head collar is the way some people react to seeing it. Many people think that a head collar is a muzzle, and they assume, therefore, that the dog might bite. While this is not necessarily a defect of the head collar, many people do find it troublesome.

Dog training with a head collar is much like training with a training collar or any other equipment. While the head collar can be an important and useful tool, it is important to use it appropriately, follow all package instructions, and to combine its use with solid training methods. The eventual goal of dog training with a head collar should be to have the dog behave as well with a regular collar as it does with the specialized head collar.

Another choice is The Dog Harness. The typical small-dog harness has a clip at the dog's back, not in front. That makes sense because a leash clip at the height of a small dog's chest puts the leash close to the ground so the dog often winds up stepping over it. Small dogs easily bruise their tracheas if they lunge forward or pull.

The Dog Harness

Chapter 5
Training Collar or Choke Collar

The basic dog training collar goes by many names, including "choke collar," "choke chain," "training collar," "correction collar," and "slip collar." These training collars (my preference for training and walking) are among the most popular and most commonly used tools with both amateur and professional dog trainers.

While a training collar is an effective tool, like any tool it must be used properly in order to be effective for you and safe for the dog. Among the most important considerations when using a training collar are:

- **How the collar fits the dog**. It is essential that the training collar be properly fitted to your dog. A properly fitted training collar is easier to use and safer for your dog.

- **Putting the training collar on properly**. There is a right way and a wrong way to fit a training collar; and putting it on wrong will make it both ineffective and potentially dangerous.

- **Using the collar properly**. A training collar should be used as a sharp reminder to the dog, not as punishment. It is important that constant pressure be avoided when using a training collar.

- **The weight of the chain and the size of the links on the training collar**. It is important that the weight of the chain be appropriate to the size and weight of the dog.

- **Placement of the collar on the dog**. It is important to properly place the collar on the dog.

The Importance of a Properly Fitted Training Collar

Determining if the training collar is the right size is relatively easy. The ideal size training collar should fit snugly, yet comfortably over the dog's head. It is important that the training collar does not fit too tightly, but it should not be too loose either.

A training collar that is too tight will be too hard to put on and off. On the other hand, a training collar that is too loose can accidentally fall off when the dog lowers its head. It is also important to know that a training collar that is too long for the dog requires a great deal of finesse to use properly. A collar that is too long can still be used, but it will require more skill on the part of the handler.

Properly Sizing and Measure the Dog for a Training Collar

It is best to measure the dog's neck with a tape measure, and then add 2 to 3 inches to that measurement. So if your dog has a neck 12" in diameter, you would want to buy a training collar that is 14" in length. Chain slip collars are generally sized in two inch increments.

Fitting the Collar Properly

When fitting a training collar, the part of the chain connected to the leash should be on the top of the dog's neck. With this type of arrangement, the collar releases the instant the leash is loosened. Training collars work by making the collar tight and loose rapidly. Tightening the collar is the first phase of the correction, and loosening it is the second phase.

If the part of the training collar that is attached to the leash is not on the top of the dog's neck, the collar can still be made tight, but it will not easily release back to a loose state. This constant pressure on the dog's neck initiates a counter response from the animal, and the dog will quickly learn to pull and strain against the leash.

Finally, it is important to purchase a well-made and strong training collar. Buying a high-quality training collar, slip, or choke collar is vital to the safety of yourself and your dog. If the worst happens, and your dog's training collar does break, it is important not to panic.

Most dogs will be unaware that they have broken the collar, at least for a few moments. In most cases, if you act as if the leash is still connected, you can probably quickly regain control of your dog. When securing a dog on the loose, the best strategy is to make a quick-slip leash by running the snap on the leash through its handle and then slipping it over the dog's head.

It may not be the best arrangement, but it will certainly do in an emergency.

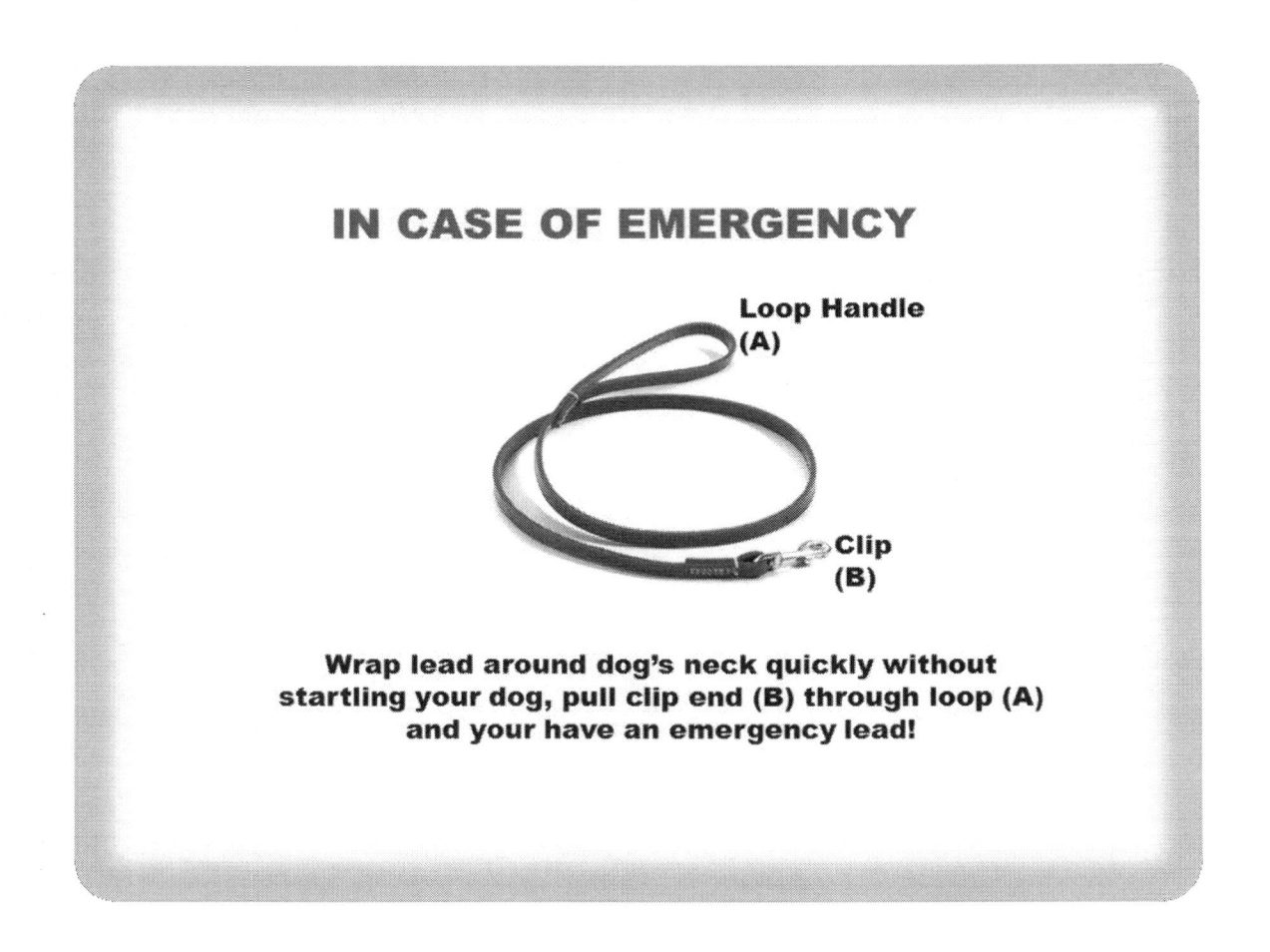

IN CASE OF EMERGENCY

Loop Handle (A)

Clip (B)

Wrap lead around dog's neck quickly without startling your dog, pull clip end (B) through loop (A) and your have an emergency lead!

Chapter 6

Reward Training

Reward training is often seen as the most modern method of training a dog, yet it is probably much older than other methods. Quite likely, reward training has been around as long as there have been dogs to train. Early humans probably used some informal kind of reward training when taming the wolf pups that eventually evolved into the various breeds of dogs around today.

Many principles of modern reward training date back decades. However, what is called "reward training" today has enjoyed its remarkable popularity only for the past 10 or 15 years. Many reward-training enthusiasts are less impressed by other methods of dog training, such as the traditional leash-and-collar. However, the best approach to training any individual dog is often a combination of leash/collar training and reward training. In addition, a training method that works perfectly for one dog may be totally inappropriate for another.

Some dogs respond wonderfully to reward training and not at all to leash and collar training, while others respond to leash/collar training and are not at all motivated by reward training. Most dogs fall somewhere in the middle of these two extremes.

Clicker training is one of the most popular forms of reward training these days.

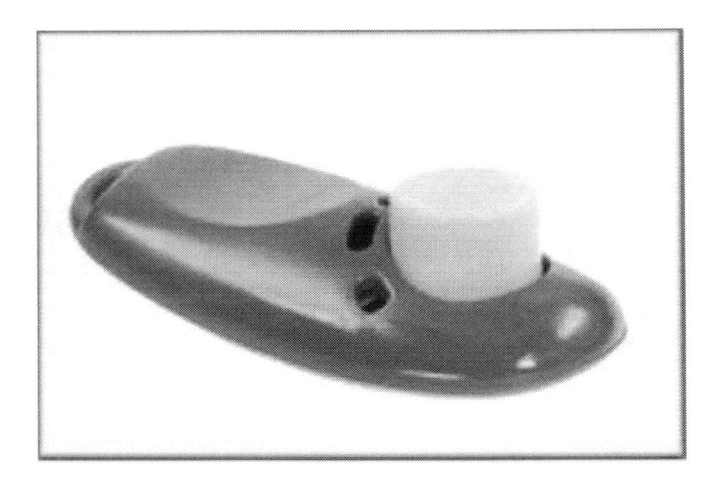

Clicker Training

While clicker training is not the answer for every dog, it can be a remarkably effective method of training many dogs. In clicker training, the dog is taught to associate a clicking sound with a reward, like a treat. The trainer clicks the clicker when the dog does something good, followed immediately by a treat.

Eventually, the dog learns to respond to the clicker alone. Most reward training uses some sort of food reward, or a reward that is associated with getting food. In most cases, complex behaviors can be taught only using this kind of positive reinforcement, and you will find that the people who train dogs for movies and television use reward training almost exclusively.

Reward training is used in all forms of dog training, including police work and military applications. Most scent detection, tracking, and police dogs are trained using some form of reward training. It is also a very effective way to teach many basic obedience commands.

Reward trainers often use bait to get their dogs into desired positions. The bait is used to get the dog to perform the desired command on his or her own and of his or her own free will. Understandably, many people look for the quickest and easiest route to training a puppy. In my experience, reward training with a treat or favorite toy is the most enjoyable and most practical way for basic training. It makes a great deal of sense to get the dog to perform the desired command without any physical intervention on the part of the handler. Getting the dog to perform a command without being touched is important.

After the dog has performed the command, she is given a reward, also called a "positive reinforcement." Treats are often used as reinforcements, but praise, such as "good boy/girl" or a pat on the head, can also be effective rewards.

Making a trained dog reliable is important, especially when the dog has an important job, like police work or drug detection, to do. For that reason, it is important to get the dog accustomed to working around distractions, and to properly socialize the animal to both people and other animals.

Many dog trainers make the mistake of training the dog only inside the house or back yard, and only when the handler is there. In order to become a reliably trained companion, the dog must be taken outside the confines of its safety zone and introduced to novel situations. It is also important to teach the dog to pay attention to the handler at all times. Having the dog's attention means having control of the dog. When used properly, reward training is very effective at getting the dog's respect and attention.

Treats and Food-Based Rewards

Training with treats and other food-based rewards is a great way to motivate your dog and speed the training process along. Most dogs are highly motivated by food rewards, and treat-training using this kind of positive reinforcement is used to train all sorts of animals, including tigers, lions, and elephants—even house cats. Before you begin a treat-based training session, however, it is a good idea to test the dog to make sure that food will motivate her through the session. Begin around the dog's regular mealtime by taking a piece of its food and waving it in front of her nose.

If she shows enthusiasm for the food, now is a great time to start the training. If the dog shows little interest or none at all, it may be best to put off the training until another time. Don't be afraid to delay the start of mealtime in order to pique the dog's interest in training. The advantages of proper training will far outweigh any delay in feeding. It is generally best to get the dog used to regular feedings, instead of leaving food out all the time. Not only does free feeding encourage the dog to overeat and increase the chances of obesity, but a free-fed dog may never be fully motivated in reward-based training.

The 'Come-When-Called' Command

Once your dog has shown interest in the offered food, it is time to begin the training. Since you already got your dog's undivided attention by showing it food, this is a great time to start. Give the dog a few pieces of food right away, and then back up a few steps. While holding the food in your hand, say "come here." When the dog comes to you, praise him effusively and give him a few pieces of food. After the dog begins to come to you easily, add a "Sit" command, and hold the collar before you give the food.

After this command is mastered, other commands, and even some tricks, can be added. Food-based positive reinforcement training is the best way to teach a variety of important commands. One good exercise is a combination of "Sit," "Stay," and "Come" commands. This can begin with the handler walking the dog, then stopping and asking her to sit.

When the dog is sitting quietly, the handler backs away and asks the dog to stay. Ideally, the dog should continue to stay until called by the handler, even if the leash is dropped. At the end of the exercise, the handler calls the dog, and when she comes to the handler, she receives food and praise.

This exercise should be repeated several times, until the dog reliably comes when called. Keep the training sessions short, especially in the beginning, as young dogs become bored easily and have a short attention span.

It is important that the dog does not consume its entire meal in the form of treats. After the dog has begins to respond regularly, the treats and food rewards can be slowly reduced. It is important to still provide these rewards, but it may no longer be necessary to provide as many. After a while, it will not be necessary to give the dog treats every single time he responds as requested. In general, it should be necessary for the dog to receive a food treat only one out of every five times he comes on command. The other four successes can be rewarded with words of praise and a rub on the neck.

Once the dog understands the basics of the "come here" command, this can be expanded, and many games can be created making great fun for handler and dog alike, as well as a great learning experience.

Some off- leash "come here" work can be introduced as well, but it is always best to start with the dog in a safe environment, such as a fenced back yard. For variety, you can try taking the dog to other safe environments.

Using Positive Reinforcement

Positive reinforcement training has long been recognized as a highly effective and enjoyable experience for both handler and dog. Positive reinforcement training is so successful, in fact, that it is the only method used to train dangerous animals such as lions and tigers for work in circuses, movies, and television industry.

Advocates of positive reinforcement swear by the effectiveness of their techniques, and it is true that the vast majority of dogs respond well to these training methods. Reward training has become increasingly popular in recent years, but, as noted earlier, chances are that some sort of reward training between humans and dogs has been going on for hundreds if not hundreds of thousands of years.

No matter what type of dog you are working with, very likely it can be helped with positive reinforcement training methods. Base your training methods on respect and trust, never on intimidation and fear. This is the only way to get the best from your dog.

Chapter 7
Crate Training

Crate training your dog may take some time and effort, but can be useful in a variety of situations. If you have a new dog or puppy, you can use the crate to limit his access to the house until he learns all the house rules—like what he can and can't chew on and where he can and can't eliminate.

Dog crates are also a safe way of transporting your dog in the car, as well as a way of taking him places where he may not be welcome to run freely. If you properly train your dog to use a dog crate, he'll think it is a safe place, and will be happy to spend time in his crate when needed.

The Crate Training Process

Crate training can take days or weeks, depending on your dog's age, temperament and past experiences. It's important to keep two things in mind while crate training. Dog crates should always be associated with something pleasant and training should take place in a series of small steps —don't go too fast.

Step One: Introduce Your Dog to the Crate

Put the dog crate in an area of your house where the family spends a lot of time, such as the family room. Put a soft blanket or towel in the crate. Bring your dog over to the crate and talk to her in a happy tone of voice.

Make sure the crate door is securely fastened opened so it won't hit your dog and frighten her.

To encourage your puppy to enter the crate, drop some small food treats near it and then just inside the door, and finally, all the way inside the crate. If she refuses to go all the way in at first, that's okay—don't force her to enter.

Continue tossing treats into the crate until your dog walks calmly all the way in to get the food. If she isn't interested in treats, try tossing a favorite toy in the crate. This step may take a few minutes or as long as several days.

Step Two: Feeding Your Dog in the Crate

After introducing your dog to the dog crate, begin feeding him his regular meals near the crate. This will create a pleasant association. If your dog readily enters the crate when you begin Step 2, put the food dish all the way at the back of the crate. If your dog is still reluctant to enter, put the dish only as far inside as he will readily go without becoming fearful or anxious. Each time you feed him, place the dish a little further back in the crate.

Once your dog is standing comfortably in the dog crate to eat his meal, you can close the door while he's eating. At first, open the door as soon as he finishes his meal. With each successive feeding, leave the door closed a few minutes longer, until he stays in for ten minutes or so after eating.

If he begins to whine to be let out, you may have increased the length of time too quickly. Next time, try leaving him in the crate for a shorter period. If he does whine or cry, it's imperative that you not let him out until he stops. Otherwise, he'll learn that the way to get out of the dog crate is to whine, so he'll keep doing it.

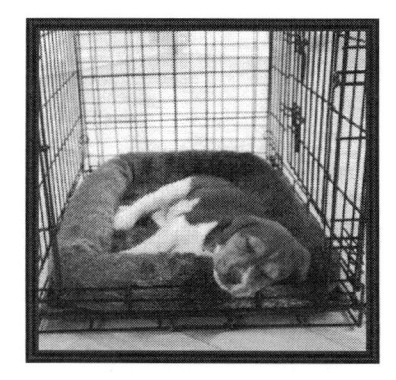

Step Three: Conditioning Your Dog for Longer Periods

After your dog is eating regular meals in the crate with no sign of fear or anxiety, you can confine her there for short periods while you're home. Call her over to the crate and give her a treat. Give her a command to enter such as, "kennel up." Encourage her by pointing to the inside of the crate with a treat in your hand.

After she enters the crate, praise her, give her the treat and close the door. Sit quietly near the crate for five to ten minutes and then go into another room for a few minutes.

Return, sit quietly again for a short time, then let her out. Repeat this process several times a day. With each repetition, gradually increase the length of time you leave her in the crate and the length of time you're out of sight.

Once your dog will stay quietly in the crate for about 30 minutes with you out of sight the majority of the time, you can begin leaving her crated when you're gone for short periods and/or letting her sleep there at night. This may take several days or several weeks.

Step Four: Crating Your Dog When Left Alone

After your dog is spending about 30 minutes in the crate without becoming anxious or afraid, you can begin leaving him crated for short periods when you leave the house.

Put him in the crate using your regular command and a treat. You might also want to leave him with a few safe toys in the crate.

Vary at what point in your "getting ready to leave" routine you put your dog in the crate.

Although he shouldn't be crated for a long time before you leave, you can crate him anywhere from five to 20 minutes prior to leaving. Make sure he has relieved himself before being crated.

Don't make your departures emotional and prolonged, but matter-of-fact. Praise your dog briefly, give him a treat for entering the crate and then leave quietly.

When you return home, don't reward your dog for excited behavior by responding to him in an excited, enthusiastic way. Keep arrivals low key.

Continue to crate your dog for short periods from time to time when you're home so she doesn't associate crating with being left alone.

Do not leave an unattended dog in the crate for more than two hours during the day.

If you need to be away for longer, either arrange for a dog sitter or leave your dog into a dog crèche.

Step Five: Crating Your Dog at Night

Put your dog in the crate using your regular command and a treat. Initially, it may be a good idea to put the crate in your bedroom or nearby in a hallway, especially if you have a puppy.

Puppies often need to go outside to eliminate during the night, and you'll want to be able to hear your puppy when he whines to be let out.

Older dogs, too, should initially be kept nearby so that crating doesn't become associated with social isolation.

Once your dog is sleeping comfortably through the night with his crate near you, you can begin to gradually move it to the location you prefer.

Step Six: Dealing with Accidents during Crate Training

It is very important to not punish the puppy or dog when it makes a mistake or has an accident during the crate-training process.

If there has been an accident, simply clean it up.

Accidents during crate training can happen until the dog has complete bowel and bladder control.

Chapter 8
House Training

House training is essential for any dog to be a valued part of the family. As with many other aspects of training, the best way to house-train a dog is to use his natural canine instincts to your benefit. The great thing about dogs—and something that can make house training much easier—is that dogs are instinctively very clean animals.

Dogs would rather not soil the areas where they sleep and eat. In addition, dogs are very good at developing habits regarding where they like to urinate and defecate. For example, dogs that are used to eliminating on concrete or gravel will prefer to eliminate there, and if used to grass, then grass would be their choice. It is possible to use these natural canine habits when house-training your dog.

Setting Up the Training Area

The first step in house training your dog is to set up your training area. A small, confined space such as a bathroom, or part of a kitchen or garage, works best. This method differs from crate training, which can be great for puppies and small dogs, but many larger dogs find a crate too confining. It is important for the handler to spend as much time as possible in the training area with the dog.

It is important for the handler to play with the dog in the training area, and to let him eat and sleep there. He should be provided with a special bed in the training area, anything from a store-bought bed to a large towel to a large box.

At first, the dog may eliminate in this area, but once he has recognized it as his own space, he will be reluctant to soil it. After the dog has got used to sleeping in the bed, you can move it around the house, relocating it from room to room. When you are not with your dog, he should be confined to the training area.

Setting Up the Toilet Area

The second part of effective house training is to set up the toilet area for your dog. Make sure she has access to this place every time she needs to eliminate. It is also important for the handler to accompany the dog each time until she gets into the habit of eliminating in the toilet area. This will ensure that the dog uses only the established toilet area.

A set feeding schedule makes house training a lot easier for both handler and dog. Feeding on a regular basis will also create a regular schedule for toilet habits. Once you know when your dog is likely to need to eliminate, it will be simple to guide him or her to the established toilet area.

Once the dog has established a toilet area and is using it on a regular basis, it is very important not to confine the dog without access to the toilet area for long periods. That is because if the dog is unable to hold it, he or she may be forced to eliminate in a different area, and this can be very stressful for the dog (not to mention for you, too!). This can make house training much more difficult for both of you.

Praise and reward the dog every time she uses the established toilet area. Never punish a dog for mistakes. Punishment will only confuse the dog and slow the house training process. House training a puppy is crucial for the well-being of both puppy and handler. The number-one reason that dogs are sent to animal shelters is because of problems with inappropriate elimination; so it is easy to see why proper house training is such an important consideration.

Given this, be sure to establish proper toilet habits when the puppy is young, since these habits can last a lifetime, and be very hard to break once established. It is very important for the handler to house-break the puppy properly.

In most cases, true house training cannot begin until the puppy is six months old. Puppies younger than this generally lack the bowel and bladder control needed for true house training. Puppies younger than six months should be confined to a small, puppy-proofed room when the handler cannot supervise them.

The entire floor of the room should be covered with newspapers or similar absorbent materials, and the paper changed every time it is soiled. As the puppy gets older, the amount of paper used can be reduced as the puppy begins to establish a preferred inside/outside toilet area. This preferred toilet area will form the basis of later house training.

Always provide the puppy with constant, unrestricted access to the established toilet area.

When you are at home, take the puppy to the toilet area every 45/60 minutes.

When you are not at home or cannot supervise the puppy, you must be sure he cannot make a "mistake." This means confining the puppy to a small area that has been thoroughly puppy-proofed. Puppy proofing a room is very similar to baby proofing a room, since puppies chew on everything.

Always provide a toilet area that does not resemble anything in your home.

Training the puppy to eliminate outside on concrete, grass, or dirt is the end game. The puppy should never be encouraged to eliminate on anything that resembles the hardwood flooring, tile or carpet he may encounter in a home.

Praise and reward your puppy every time she eliminates in the established toilet area. The puppy must learn to associate toileting in the established areas with good things, like treats, toys and praise from her handler.

Always keep a set schedule when feeding your puppy, and provide constant access to fresh, clean drinking water. A consistent feeding schedule equals a consistent toilet schedule. Using a crate can be a big help in training a puppy to develop self-control.

The idea behind crate training is that the puppy will not want to toilet in his bed so you must be present to allow him out to pee and/or poop every 45 minutes initially, extending the period until the puppy has complete bowel and bladder control.

When you know your puppy is about to pee, say the word "pee pee." Your puppy will associate this command when it is peeing. Give lots of praise as the dog is peeing, and hand him a treat when finished. Now, while you may think this is over the top, it is an effective way to train a dog to pee on command, and be comfortable going to the toilet in front of you. It also gives you peace of mind knowing your dog has peed before you go to bed, set off on a journey with the dog, or have to leave him alone while you step out for a while.

Finally, it is important to be patient when house training a puppy. House training can take as long as several months, but it is much easier to house train right the first time than to retrain a problem dog.

A Trained Dog Is A Happy Dog!

Epilogue
Leader of the Pack

The importance of training and introducing your puppy or dog to different people, places, noises, car travel (e.g., in a crate) and other animals cannot be overstated.

As soon as your dog is collar-and-leash trained, is fully vaccinated, take him out daily to enjoy all the wonderful smells and sights. Familiarize him/her with your local vet and groomers, and attend dog training classes if possible.

Stick with the rules, play and love your new canine friend. Just as a child looks to his or her parents for guidance and boundaries, so does your dog. Sometimes we have to use tough love, but in the long run, you and your dog will be happier if you maintain your role as Leader of The Pack.

**Finnish Spitz "Ihana-Ilotulitus of Storm Valley" (Hannah)
Owned and loved by Trish Foster.**

Appendix

History of the Dog

The Grey Wolf

The domestic dog is a subspecies of the grey wolf, a member of the *Canidae* family of the mammalian order Carnivore. The term "domestic dog" is generally used for both domesticated and feral varieties. The dog may have been the first animal to be domesticated, and has been the most widely kept working, hunting, and pet animal in human history.

The word "dog" may also mean the male of a species, as opposed to the word "bitch" for females. The present lineage of dogs was domesticated from grey wolves about 15,000 years ago.

Though remains of domesticated dogs have been found in Siberia and Belgium from about 33,000 years ago, none of those lineages seem to have survived the Last Glacial Maximum.

Although DNA testing suggests an evolutionary split between dogs and wolves around 100,000 years ago, no specimens prior to 33,000 years ago are clearly morphologically domesticated dog. By nature, every dog looks to the pack leader for guidance.

The basis of all good dog training, including reward-based training, is for the handler to set him or herself up as the pack leader. The pack leader is more than just the dominant dog, or the one who tells all the subordinates what to do.

More important, the pack leader provides leadership and protection, and his or her leadership is vital to the success, survival, and well-being of the pack.

Made in the USA
Charleston, SC
20 June 2013